# STECK-VAUGHN STUDY SKILLS FOR ADULTS

## Using Resources

## Contents

| | | |
|---|---|---|
| LESSON 1 | Locating Entry Words in a Dictionary | 2 |
| LESSON 2 | Understanding Dictionary Entries | 4 |
| LESSON 3 | Using the Parts of a Book | 8 |
| LESSON 4 | Using a Book's Index | 12 |
| LESSON 5 | Finding Topics in an Encyclopedia | 16 |
| LESSON 6 | Using an Encyclopedia's Index | 20 |
| LESSON 7 | Getting to Know Your Library | 22 |
| LESSON 8 | Choosing and Comparing Resources | 26 |
| REVIEW | Using Dictionaries and Book Parts | 30 |
| REVIEW | Using Encyclopedias | 31 |
| REVIEW | Using Library Resources | 32 |
| ANSWER KEY | | Inside Back Cover |

## Acknowledgments

Executive Editor: Diane Sharpe
Supervising Editor: Stephanie Muller
Design Manager: Laura Cole
Cover Designer: D. Childress/Alan Klemp

Product Development: Curriculum Concepts, Inc.
Writer: Joan L. Poole

**Illustrators**: pp. 22, 24 Janet Bohn; pp. 15, 17, 18 Pam Carroll; pp. 5, 6, 10, 21 Nancy Didion; p. 29 Toby Gowing; p. 2 Al Hering; p. 26 Michael McDermott
**Photography**: cover © Carr Clifton/Allstock

ISBN 0-8114-2526-6

Copyright © 1994 Steck-Vaughn Company.
All rights reserved. No part of the material protected by this copyright may be reproduced or utilized in any form or by any means, electronic or mechanical, including photocopying, recording, or by any information storage and retrieval system, without permission in writing from the copyright owner. Requests for permission to make copies of any part of the work should be mailed to: Copyright Permissions, Steck-Vaughn Company, P.O. Box 26015, Austin, TX 78755. Printed in the United States of America.

1 2 3 4 5 6 7 8 9 0 CCG 00 99 98 97 96 95 94

STECK-VAUGHN COMPANY
A Subsidiary of National Education Corporation

## LESSON 1

# Locating Entry Words in a Dictionary

Important resources, such as the dictionary and the encyclopedia, have entry words or topics, arranged in **alphabetical order.** Understanding alphabetical order will make locating entry words easy.

## Ask Yourself

Do you know how to put entry words in alphabetical order? Number the list of entry words below according to alphabetical order.

_____ dapple

_____ vaquero

_____ mesa

_____ Albert Einstein

_____ Ferris wheel

_____ carbon dioxide

_____ French horn

_____ Dutch

_____ Mount Everest

_____ bonsai

Did you have any trouble alphabetizing the entry words? If so, this lesson will teach you how to look up words in a dictionary, including names, places, and compound words.

## How To

### Locate Entry Words in a Dictionary

- Imagine that your dictionary is divided into three sections: the front (A–F), the middle (G–P), and the back (Q–Z). Open to the correct section.
- Look at the pair of guide words at the top outer corner of each page. The guide words tell the first and last entry word on a page.
- Use the guide words and alphabetical order to locate an entry word.
- Look up people's names under their last, or family, name.
- Look up names of places under the particular, not the general, word in the name. For example, *Lake Victoria* would be under *Victoria*, not *Lake*.
- Notice that dictionaries often list biographical names and geographical places in alphabetical order in separate sections.
- Locate compound words under the first letter of the first word.
- If you still can't find the entry word, check to see if it appears as a related word form. For example, you would find *happiest* in the entry for *happy*.

## Try It Out

For each of the following entry words, circle the letter under which the entry would be alphabetized. Refer to the **How To** box for hints. The first one has been done for you.

1. ⓢacred cow
2. fly ball
3. North Sea
4. Bay of Fundy
5. French fries
6. Anne Frank
7. weather station
8. Great Barrier Reef
9. bullet train

## What Have I Learned?

Suppose that Kristina is having trouble finding the following words in her dictionary: *funniest*, *Pablo Casals*, *Guatemala City*, and *Grand Canyon*. Suggest four steps she can take to find these words.

_____
_____
_____
_____

# LESSON 2: Understanding Dictionary Entries

Although many words have only one meaning, others may have several meanings. To find the definition you need, read and compare all the definitions given. Then use context clues and example sentences to find the correct meaning.

## Ask Yourself

Can you use context clues to determine the meaning of a word? Each sentence below uses the word *bond* differently. Read each sentence. Then read the definitions. Beside each sentence, write the letter of the best definition. Circle any words in the sentences that helped you determine the meaning.

1. There is a strong bond of friendship between us. _____
2. Joe bought a $1000 savings bond from the government. _____
3. The guard tied a rope bond around the criminal's wrists. _____
4. The accused person was released on $100,000 bond. _____

a. something that fastens things together

b. a uniting force or influence

c. a certificate for which the government agrees to pay money back with interest at a future date

d. an amount of money an accused person must pay if he or she does not appear for trial

Did context clues help you determine the meaning of *bond* in each sentence?

## How To

### Choose the Correct Definition

- If an entry word has more than one definition, read and compare all the meanings. The dictionary numbers the different meanings for you.
- If an entry word is a **homograph**—a word that is spelled the same way as another word but has a totally different meaning—the dictionary gives each meaning a separate entry. For example, **tear**$^1$ (meaning "rip") and **tear**$^2$ (meaning "teardrop") are homographs that have separate entries.
- Read any example phrases and sentences that the dictionary provides. They show how a word is used in context. These are called **context clues.**
- Use context clues to find the meaning that fits your sentence.

# Try It Out

Read the following dictionary entries. Then choose the meaning that fits in each sentence. If the entry word has more than one meaning, write the number of the correct meaning beside the sentence. If the word is a homograph, write the number that is beside the entry word. Refer to the **How To** box for hints.

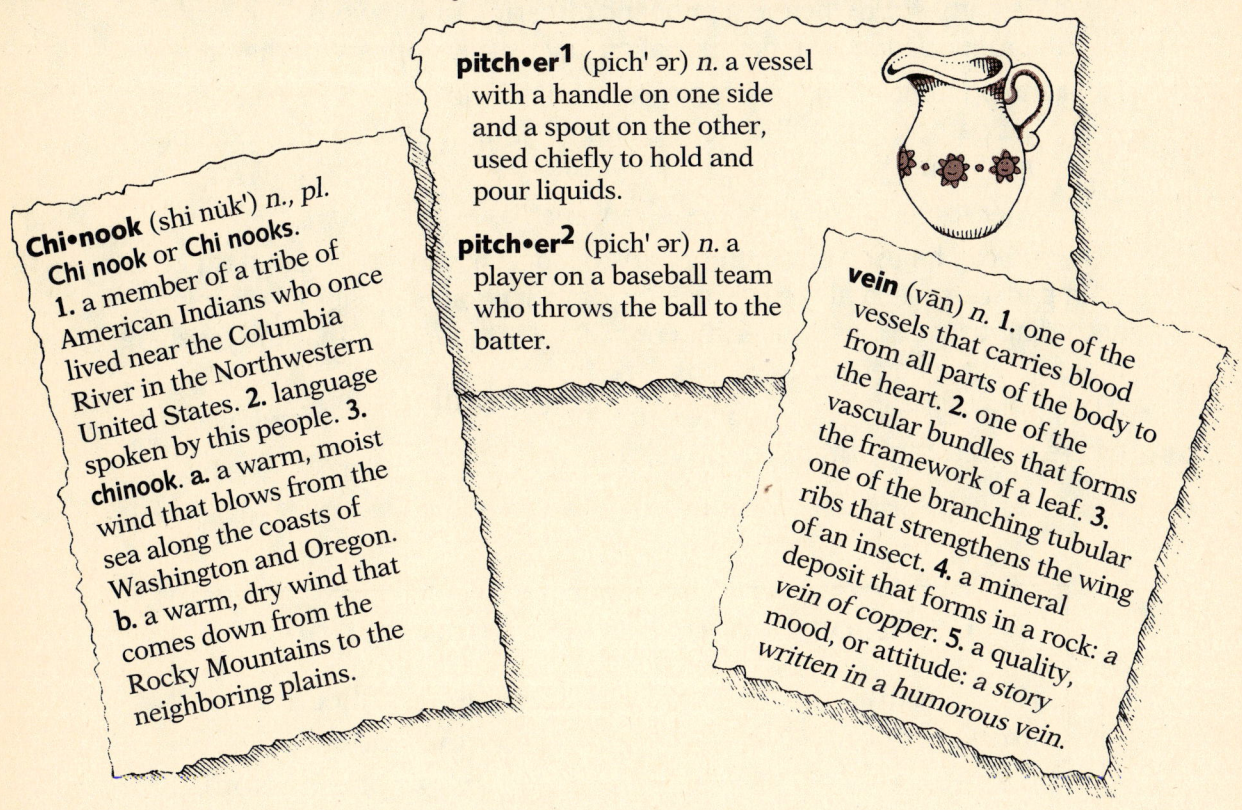

**pitch•er¹** (pich' ər) *n.* a vessel with a handle on one side and a spout on the other, used chiefly to hold and pour liquids.

**pitch•er²** (pich' ər) *n.* a player on a baseball team who throws the ball to the batter.

**Chi•nook** (shi nŭk') *n., pl.* **Chi nook** or **Chi nooks**. 1. a member of a tribe of American Indians who once lived near the Columbia River in the Northwestern United States. 2. language spoken by this people. 3. **chinook. a.** a warm, moist wind that blows from the sea along the coasts of Washington and Oregon. **b.** a warm, dry wind that comes down from the Rocky Mountains to the neighboring plains.

**vein** (vān) *n.* 1. one of the vessels that carries blood from all parts of the body to the heart. 2. one of the vascular bundles that forms the framework of a leaf. 3. one of the branching tubular ribs that strengthens the wing of an insect. 4. a mineral deposit that forms in a rock: a vein of copper. 5. a quality, mood, or attitude: a story written in a humorous vein.

1. Traders and Native Americans in the Pacific Northwest spoke a mixture of Chinook, other American Indian languages, French, and English. _____

2. When the chinook blows down from the mountains to the plains in spring, the river begins to thaw. _____

3. The pitcher for the New York Yankees had such a wicked curve ball, he struck out three batters in a row. _____

4. Carole placed a sugar bowl and a pitcher of milk on the table. _____

5. What would you do if you discovered a vein of gold in that rock? _____

6. The jugular vein carries blood from your head and neck to your heart. _____

7. Was your conversation in a serious or a humorous vein? _____

8. If you hold the oak leaf up to the light, you will see each vein. _____

# How To

## Locate Other Parts of a Dictionary Entry

- Each boldfaced entry word may be divided with • to show separate syllables. After the entry word, there is a **phonetic** respelling of the word. This is the word's pronunciation. The pronunciation key usually appears on the same page.
- After the pronunciation, look for an abbreviation in slanted, or **italic,** type. It tells what part of speech the word is and whether it is plural. For example, *n., pl.* means "noun, plural."
- Then other forms of the word are given, such as *rest, rested, resting*.
- If a word can be used as different parts of speech, there will be a dash before each part-of-speech abbreviation. This dash separates groups of meanings according to their part of speech. For example, —*adj.* tells that the meanings that follow are adjectives.
- Word histories, called **etymologies,** are shown in brackets. Etymologies tell where a word came from and what it originally meant.

### Common Part-of-Speech Abbreviations

| | | | |
|---|---|---|---|
| *n.* | noun | *adj.* | adjective |
| *pron.* | pronoun | *adv.* | adverb |
| *v.* | verb | *prep.* | preposition |
| *v.t.* | transitive verb | *conj.* | conjunction |
| *v.i.* | intransitive verb | *contr.* | contraction |

## Try It Out

Read the following dictionary entries. Then answer the questions on the next page. Look at the **How To** boxes and the abbreviation key for hints.

**bass**¹ (bās) *n., pl.* **bass•es. 1.** a male singing voice with the deepest and lowest range. **2.** a male singer who has such a voice. **3.** a musical instrument with a similar range. **4.** a musical part for such a voice or instrument. —*adj.* **1.** able to sing or play the bass: *a bass voice, a bass clarinet.* **2.** for the bass. [From the Latin word *bassus,* meaning "low, short."]

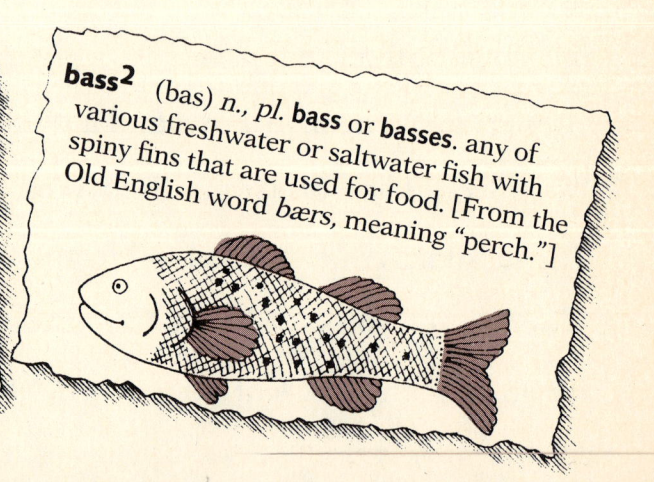

**bass**² (bas) *n., pl.* **bass** or **basses.** any of various freshwater or saltwater fish with spiny fins that are used for food. [From the Old English word *bærs,* meaning "perch."]

1. Is *bass* a homograph? _____

2. Do the two dictionary entries for *bass* have the same phonetic respelling, or pronunciation? _____

3. Locate the definition that describes the kind of *bass* that is played in a jazz band. Give the number of the entry word and the number of the definition.
_____

   What did this word originally mean in Latin? _____

4. Find the meaning that describes the kind of *bass* that people eat. What part of speech is it? _____

   What language did this word come from, and what did it originally mean?____
_____

5. What part of speech is *bass* in the sentence "Richard plays bass guitar"? _____
_____

6. What does the abbreviation *adj.* mean? _____
_____

7. What is a plural form of the word *bass*? _____

## What Have I Learned?

Words such as *dude* or *video* are in the dictionary, but the definitions may not make sense in a sentence used today. How would you explain to a classmate why she cannot find the correct meaning for these words in an older dictionary?

_____
_____
_____
_____
_____
_____

## LESSON 3
# Using the Parts of a Book

When selecting and comparing books, always look at their different parts. **Title** and **copyright** pages tell the book's title, author, illustrator, and publisher, as well as the place and date of publication. A **table of contents** lists units, chapters, articles, stories, and other features in a book. A **glossary** defines special or difficult terms. An **index** tells where to find specific topics.

## Ask Yourself

How often do you use the parts of a book? Look at the title and copyright pages below. Then answer the questions.

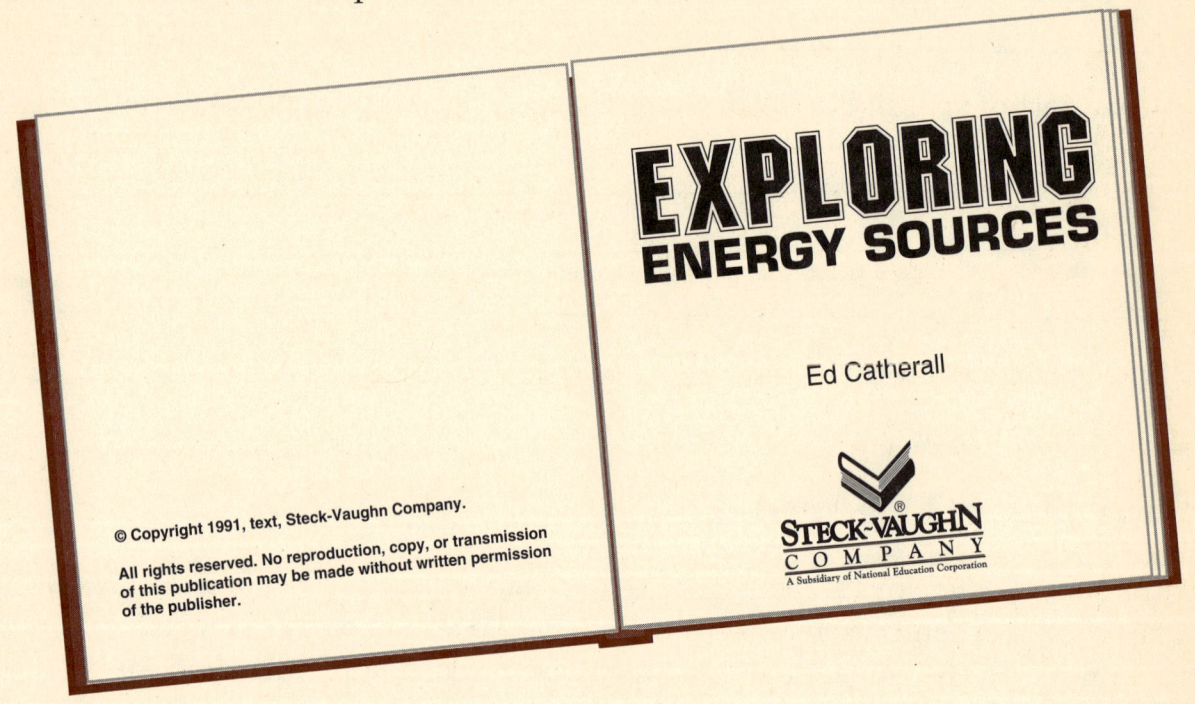

# EXPLORING
## ENERGY SOURCES

Ed Catherall

**STECK-VAUGHN COMPANY**
A Subsidiary of National Education Corporation

© Copyright 1991, text, Steck-Vaughn Company.

All rights reserved. No reproduction, copy, or transmission of this publication may be made without written permission of the publisher.

1. Who is the author of this book? _____
2. Who is the publisher? _____
3. Does the title page name an illustrator? _____
4. When was this book published? _____

Were you able to answer the questions about title and copyright information? If not, you may need to learn more about using book parts.

## How To

### Use the Parts of a Book

- Check the **title page** to find the title, author, illustrator, and publisher.
- Use the **copyright page** to find the date of publication and whether there were any previous editions. A recent copyright date means that a book's information is up-to-date. This helps you compare books and choose the most current one. Sometimes the title and copyright information is combined on one page.
- Look to see whether a book has a **glossary** in the back. Glossaries appear mostly in nonfiction books. Use a glossary to locate the meaning of difficult terms you come across in a book.

## Try It Out

**A.** Choose three of your favorite books. Include both fiction and nonfiction. Check to see which book parts they contain. For each book, complete the chart. Use the **How To** box for hints.

|  | Book 1 | Book 2 | Book 3 |
|---|---|---|---|
| **TITLE PAGE** |  |  |  |
| *Book Title* |  |  |  |
| *Author's Name* |  |  |  |
| *Illustrator's Name* |  |  |  |
| *Publishing Company* |  |  |  |
| *Place of Publication* |  |  |  |
| **COPYRIGHT PAGE** |  |  |  |
| *Copyright Date* |  |  |  |
| *Previous Editions* |  |  |  |
| **TABLE OF CONTENTS** (page number) |  |  |  |
| **GLOSSARY** (page number) |  |  |  |

**B.** Use this part of a glossary to answer the questions. Refer to the **How To** box for hints.

> **fats** Chemical substances found in animals and plants. They are solid and contain carbon, hydrogen, and oxygen.
>
> **ferment** Usually, this means to break down sugars and other carbohydrates into alcohol, using small organisms (living things) called yeast, which digest the substances.
>
> **fuel** Material from which energy can be released to give heat, usually by burning.
>
> **geologist** A scientist who studies the development of Earth's crust.
>
> **geyser** A spring that spouts hot water into the air.

1. What does a geologist study? _____
2. What kind of water does a geyser release into the air? _____
3. What does *ferment* mean? Use your own words.
   _____
4. Where do you find fats? _____
5. How is a glossary like a dictionary?
   _____
   _____

   How is it different?
   _____
   _____

## ✓ How To

### Use a Table of Contents

- Locate the table of contents at the beginning of a book, after the title and copyright pages.
- Skim the titles of the chapters, sections, units, articles, or stories to find what the book contains.
- Use the page numbers to find specific chapters, sections, units, articles, or stories.
- Check to see whether the table of contents lists special features, such as interviews, summaries, explanatory notes, or additional reading suggestions.

## Try It Out

Use the section from the table of contents to answer the questions.

### Unit 6    Africa South of the Sahara
Africa Remembered    *A former slave describes his capture and rescue* ............................................. 68
The Hour of Triumph    *Ghana's first leader announces his country's independence* .................. 72
A Life Apart    *A young South African woman talks about life under apartheid* ....................... 74

### Unit 7    South Asia
An American Reporter Meets Gandhi    *The famous Indian leader explains his philosophy* .......... 80
Daughter of Destiny    *Benazir Bhutto, former prime minister of Pakistan, remembers her childhood* ............... 84

### Unit 8    The Far East
Japan Meets the West    *A Japanese man describes learning the ABC's* ........................................ 88
The War Years in Vietnam    *A Vietnamese woman remembers her father* ................................. 90
The Red Guards    *A Chinese woman recalls the horror of the Cultural Revolution* ....................... 94

1. Which unit would tell about Ghana's independence? _____

2. If you wanted to know what it is like for a Japanese person to learn English, which chapter would you read? Give the title and page number.

   _____

3. Which page would you turn to if you were writing a report about slavery?

   _____

4. To get a first-person account of the Vietnam War, which chapter would you read? Give the title and page number. _____

5. To find information about South African laws designed to keep blacks and whites apart, which chapter would you read? Give the title and page number.

   _____

6. What special feature does this table of contents have?

   _____

## What Have I Learned?

Imagine that you have been asked to give an oral report about a famous freedom fighter. Choose someone who interests you, such as Mohandas Gandhi, Sojourner Truth, Tecumseh, or Frederick Douglass. On your own paper, describe how you would use the parts of different resource books to make your selection.

## LESSON 4
# Using a Book's Index

The quickest way to find information in a nonfiction book is to use the book's index. It lists the specific topics and subtopics in the book and gives the page numbers on which each topic can be found.

## Ask Yourself

How much do you know about using a book's index? Decide whether the following statements are true or false. Beside each statement, write T or F.

1. An index lists topics and subtopics in the order in which they happened.
   _____

2. Every fiction and nonfiction book has an index. _____

3. An index usually comes at the beginning of a book, after the copyright page.
   _____

4. Sometimes an index tells whether a topic is illustrated by the author. _____

5. An index tells the meaning of special terms in a book. _____

Do you think all the statements are false? Read the **How To** box to make sure.

## ✓ How To

### Use a Book's Index

- Before using an index, identify your topic word.
- Locate an index in the back of a nonfiction book.
- Notice that the index gives an alphabetical listing of the book's main topics and subtopics.
- Then search the index for your topic word in alphabetical order.
- Check any subtopics for more specific information.
- Look up most people's names under their last name.
- Check to see whether the index lists maps, photographs, and pictures of topics.

## Try It Out

Use this excerpt from an index to answer the questions below. Refer to the **How To** box for hints.

# INDEX

Mandela, Nelson, 77. *See also,*
    South Africa
Maoris, 105, *illus.*
maps
    historical
        Ancient Civilizations, 2
        Ancient Greece and Rome, 14
        Inca Empire, 111
    political
        Palestine Today, 57
        South African Homelands, 75
    regional
        Africa South of the Sahara, 66
        Americas, 108
        Australia and New Zealand, 100
        Eastern Europe, 38
        Far East, 86
        North Africa, 50
        South Asia, 78
        Western Europe, 24
    route
        Napoleon in Russia, 33
Mesopotamia, 4
Mexican Revolution, 118-121

1. How many main topics are there in this section of the index? _____

2. How many subtopics can you find under the main topic *maps*? _____

3. Does this index include sub-subtopics? _____

4. On which page would you find information about Nelson Mandela? _____

5. On which page would you find a map of Napoleon's route through Russia? _____

6. If you were writing a report about political conditions in South Africa, which map would help you? Give its name and page number. _____

7. If you were writing a report about Canada, which regional map might help you? Give its name and page number. _____

13

## How To

### Find Related Topics in an Index

- To locate additional information about a topic, use the **cross-references** in the index. In a cross-reference, the phrase *See also* is in italic type after the main topic. Here the index lists other topics that are related to your topic.
- Look under the listing of related topics for the specific information you want.
- Think of additional topic words that might contain information on your topic. Check to see if they are listed in the index.

## Try It Out

**A.** Review the index on page 13. Then answer the questions below. Refer to the *How To* box for hints.

1. Which topic word is followed by a cross-reference?

   _____

2. What does this reference tell you to do?

   _____

   _____

3. Will this section of the index have the information you need to follow the directions in the cross-reference?

   _____

**B.** William is trying to find answers to the following questions. He has chosen a topic word for each question, but that word is not in the index. For each question, suggest another topic word that he could look up. Refer to the *How To* box for hints.

1. Who invented the light bulb? William's topic word is *bulb*. He should check

   under _____

2. What was Harriet Tubman's involvement with the Underground Railroad?

   William's topic word is *railroad*. He should check under _____

   _____

14

3. When was the Prince Edward Island National Park founded? William's topic word is *Edward*. He should check under _____

4. What is the largest industry in Baja California Sur? William's topic word is *Sur*. He should check under _____

5. How are Asian elephants trained to work in the logging industry? William's topic word is *Asian*. He should check under _____

## What Have I Learned?

Suppose that you are writing a paper about two kinds of poisonous snakes—rattlesnakes and copperheads. You find a book called *Snakes That Bite* with a great photograph on the cover. You want to use the book's index to see whether it actually contains information on your topic. Suggest specific topics and subtopics to look for in the index.

**RATTLESNAKE**

**COPPERHEAD**

## LESSON 5

# Finding Topics in an Encyclopedia

The encyclopedia is one of the most convenient and complete sources of information you can use. This book or set of books contains articles on people, places, events, and many other topics. Use the guide letters on encyclopedia volumes and the guide words on encyclopedia pages to search for topics.

## Ask Yourself

Do you know where and how to find information about certain topics? Read the following questions. Then circle the letter of the answer you think is correct.

1. To learn the origin of the word *Minnesota*, which source would you choose?

    **a.** an encyclopedia      **b.** a dictionary      **c.** a newspaper

2. To find facts about killer whales, which source would be the best choice?

    **a.** an encyclopedia      **b.** a dictionary      **c.** a newspaper

3. To find the causes of the French and Indian War, which source would you choose?

    **a.** an encyclopedia      **b.** a dictionary      **c.** a newspaper

4. To find out about an important event that happened last week, which source would you choose?

    **a.** an encyclopedia      **b.** a dictionary      **c.** a newspaper

5. To find facts about the city of Paris, France, in an encyclopedia, what would you look up in order to get the most information?

    **a.** both *Paris* and *France*      **b.** just *Paris*      **c.** just *France*

6. Both encyclopedias and dictionaries arrange information in what kind of order?

    **a.** alphabetical      **b.** numeric      **c.** chronological

7. Which of the following features is not found in an encyclopedia?

    **a.** guide words      **b.** guide letters      **c.** example sentences

Were you sure about your answers to the questions above? If not, read on to learn more about locating topics in an encyclopedia.

# How To

**Find Topics in an Encyclopedia**

- Select the topic word or words that best describe your topic.
- Locate most people's names under the last name.
- Locate most geographical names under the first letter of the most particular word of the name.
- Match the guide letters on encyclopedia volumes with the first letters of your topic word. For the topic word *Alaska*, choose Volume A.
- Use the guide words at the top of each left-hand and right-hand page. They tell the first and last topic on those two pages.
- Use the guide words and alphabetical order to locate your topic.
- To find related topics, look for any cross-references at the end of encyclopedia articles.

# Try It Out

**A.** To find information on each of the following topics, which topic word would you look up in an encyclopedia? Circle one topic word for each question. Then tell why you chose that word instead of the others. Refer to the *How To* box for hints.

1. When did American lecturer Helen Keller live?

    Helen      Keller      lecturer

    _____

    _____

2. What kind of plant is an orchid?

    flower      orchid      plant

    _____

    _____

3. What birds make their nest in the Gaspé Peninsula?

    Peninsula      Gaspé      birds

    _____

    _____

17

**B.** Between which two guide words would you find each of the following topics? Write the letter of the correct guide words beside each topic. Refer to the **How To** box for hints.

　　_____ 1. Vancouver Island　　　　a. **Milan/Millay, Edna St. Vincent**

　　_____ 2. Israel　　　　　　　　　 b. **Vancouver/vandals**

　　_____ 3. The Milky Way　　　　　 c. **elephant/elevator**

　　_____ 4. Grandma Moses　　　　　 d. **Moscow/mosque**

　　_____ 5. elephant seal　　　　　 e. **Islam/Italian Architecture**

## How To

**Research a Topic Thoroughly**

- To find additional information about a topic, look up more than one topic word in the encyclopedia.
- Think of other topic words that might contain information related to your topic.
- Look for cross-references at the end of encyclopedia articles. They refer to other articles that have related information.

## Try It Out

For each of the following questions, think of two or more topic words that you could look up in an encyclopedia to find the answer. Refer to the **How To** box for hints.

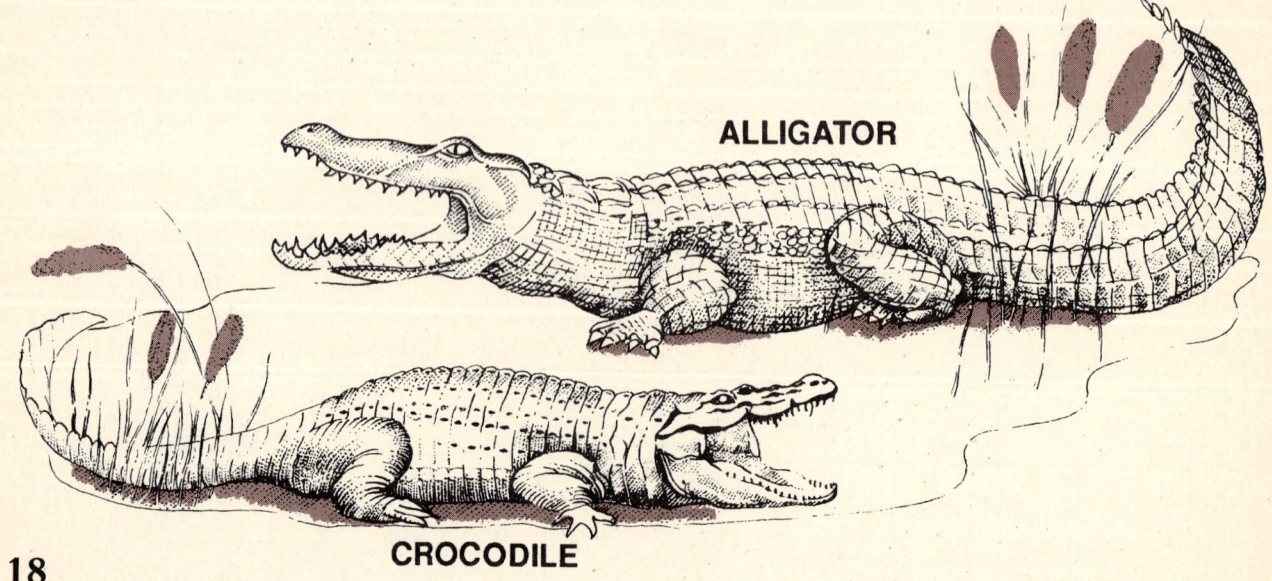

**ALLIGATOR**

**CROCODILE**

**1.** How do alligators differ from crocodiles?

_____

_____

**2.** What is the largest mammal? Where does it live?

_____

**3.** What were the causes of the Civil War?

_____

**4.** In what ways are people harming the environment?

_____

**5.** Scientists once believed that the sun revolved around the earth. What changed their minds?

_____

## What Have I Learned?

Select one of the questions in the *Try It Out* exercise above. Look up your topic words in an encyclopedia. Then write down three or more facts from the articles.

**TOPIC WORDS:** _____

**FACTS:** _____

_____

_____

_____

_____

_____

_____

_____

_____

## LESSON 6: Using an Encyclopedia's Index

Sometimes a single encyclopedia article will not give enough information. But an encyclopedia often contains information related to your topic in other articles. Sometimes these articles are about topics you might not think of on your own. If you are unsure about which other topic words to check, use the index. This is often a separate volume that lists all the topics covered in the encyclopedia.

## Ask Yourself

The main topics below are followed by lists of additional articles. If you think an article might have information on the main topic, write yes. If not, write no.

**Ganges River**

Asia _____

January (Special Days) _____

Religion _____

Rivers _____

**Garbage**

Flies _____

Middle Ages _____

Waste Disposal _____

**Polo, Marco**

Exploration _____

Geography _____

Glasses _____

**Ice Cream (History)**

Indonesia _____

Money _____

Trade _____

Did you write no for any of the topics? Surprise! All of the topics are related.

## How To

### Use an Encyclopedia's Index

- An encyclopedia's index is usually a separate volume that lists the main topics and related topics in alphabetical order.
- Use an encyclopedia's index to find articles listed under your main topics.
- Locate your main topic in the index, and skim the related topics.
- Find the volume and page number references in dark type, after each topic. The reference **A:24** means an article is in Volume A on page 24.
- Check to see if the index lists any illustrations related to your topic. For example, a topic might be followed by the words *with portrait*.

## Try It Out

Use this section from an encyclopedia's index to answer the questions below. Refer to the **How To** box for hints.

> **Environmental Pollution E:300**
> *with pictures*
> Diseases **D:232**
> Ecology **E:50**
> Recycling **R:186**
> Weather (Effects on) **W:162**
> Wildlife Conservation (Value of) **W:305–306**

1. Does the encyclopedia article about environmental pollution have any pictures?

2. In which volume and on which page would you find a related article about recycling?

3. What would you expect to learn about pollution from the article about wildlife conservation?

4. What aspect of pollution would you expect to read about in the article on weather?

## What Have I Learned?

Choose one of the following topics: polar bears, poisonous snakes, giant clams, buffalo, kangaroos, or vultures. Make a list of related articles that you would expect to find in an encyclopedia's index. How does your list compare with the encyclopedia's index in your library?

# LESSON 7
# Getting to Know Your Library

Take advantage of the wide number of resources available at your school or community library. Whether you locate information through a card catalog or on a computer, understanding and using all library resources will improve the quality of your schoolwork. It will also make any research you do easier and more enjoyable.

## Ask Yourself

How familiar are you with library resources? For each question on the next page, write the resource you think would help you find the answer.

Which resources would you choose to:

1. get information about a gymnast who won a gold medal in the last Olympics? _____
2. obtain a list of books about South Africa? _____
3. learn about the Vietnam War? _____
4. get a list of magazine articles published within the last three years about home computers? _____
5. read magazine articles themselves? _____
6. read a newspaper published in 1962? _____
7. find a videotape about how to play tennis? _____
8. find a book entitled *The Endless Steppe*? _____
9. find out what books have been published on the subject of hiking? _____
10. find out what books have been written by the author Richard Peck? _____

Does your school library have all of these resources? Does your local library?

# How To

### Get the Most out of Your Library

- Spend time at your library so that you know what kinds of resources it offers.
- Practice using the card catalog to look up books that interest you. The card catalog lists nonfiction books in alphabetical order by title, author, and subject.
- Check to see if your library has a computer that can help you search for titles, authors, and subjects even faster.
- Locate the periodical shelves to find out what magazines and newspapers your library has.
- Find out whether your library stores newspapers, magazines, and other materials on strips of film, called "microfilm," or sheets of film, called microfiche.
- Keep track of any new materials and tools, such as videotapes, your library purchases. Find out from your librarian how to use them.

## Try It Out

Visit your school or local library to find out what resources are available to you. Take the following questionnaire with you. With a librarian's help, answer the following questions.

1. What resources does your library have to locate a list of magazine articles about recycling?
   _____

2. Where is the card catalog located? _____

   Is it in card or book form? _____

   How would you use the card catalog to look up the book *The Phantom Tollbooth*? _____
   _____

3. Does your library have any computers? _____

   If so, what kind are they? _____

   Would they help you locate book titles, authors, and subjects? _____

   Would they allow you to read a newspaper article on the computer screen? _____

4. Does your library have audiotapes, filmstrips, or videotapes? _____

   Where are they located? _____

   How are they arranged? _____

   How do you use them? _____

5. What kinds of magazines and newspapers does your library have? _____
   _____

   Where are they located? _____

   Are any stored on microfilm or microfiche? ____

   Where are the machines for viewing microfilm and microfiche located? _____

## How To

**Get Help from Your Librarian**

- Always ask your librarian for help if you cannot find what you need.
- Have a clear idea of what you are looking for before you go to the library. Write down titles, authors, and topics if you know them.
- Explain to the librarian what you want to find.
- Ask for help with special equipment, such as machines for viewing microfilm or computers for learning skills or playing video games.
- Visit your library often. The more you use it, the more you will be able to find and use resources on your own.

## Try It Out

Now that you have visited your library, go back to your answers to *Ask Yourself* on page 23. Make any changes or additions based on what you have just learned.

_____
_____
_____
_____
_____

## What Have I Learned?

Make a list of different kinds of library resources. Give examples of how each resource can be used.

_____
_____
_____
_____
_____
_____
_____
_____

## LESSON 8

# Choosing and Comparing Resources

As you get to know your library, familiarize yourself with the special features of different resources. Compare the resources carefully to choose the best one for a particular project.

## Ask Yourself

Suppose you were doing research about Mark Twain and made a list of topics to research. Would you be able to locate the best resources? For each numbered topic, write the name of one resource you would choose.

almanac          magazine
atlas            newspaper
dictionary       fiction book
encyclopedia     nonfiction book

1. Detailed information about the life of Mark Twain
   _____

2. The correct pronunciation and spelling of Mark Twain's name
   _____

3. A map of the state of Missouri, where Twain was born
   _____

4. Information about the history of Missouri
   _____

5. An article about present-day life in Missouri
   _____

Did you have trouble deciding on the best resource for any of the topics? Remember, you can't always find everything you need in just one place.

26

# How To

**Choose Among Resources**

- Choose an almanac for a quick answer to a specific question, such as "Who won the World Series in 1986?" Published every year, an almanac gives facts and figures about current events and other subjects.
- Select an atlas when you need a map. The title of the atlas tells the kind of maps it contains, and the index helps you find specific maps.
- Choose an encyclopedia if you need summaries of information on people, places, events, and other general topics.
- Choose a dictionary to look up a word's meaning, spelling, pronunciation, or history.
- Use the *Readers' Guide to Periodical Literature* to find lists of magazine articles on a specific subject. This guide lists articles by author and subject with the magazine's name, date, and page numbers.

## Try It Out

Imagine that you had to research two topics from the list below. Describe which resources you would choose, and tell what you would hope to find. Refer to the **How To** box for hints.

The tallest building in the world
A map of Paris
All the articles on the albatross published in 1993
Who won the World Cup in 1982?
The location of the Persian Gulf
The history of the name *Texas*

**TOPIC 1:** _____

_____

_____

**TOPIC 2:** _____

_____

_____

## How To

**Compare Different Resources**

- Leaf through a source to see how much detail it contains. Is it too detailed or too brief? A nonfiction book about your topic will be much more detailed than an encyclopedia entry.
- Check copyright dates on all sources to see if the information is current.
- Choose a source that you can read easily—one that isn't too simple or too difficult.

## Try It Out

Answer the following questions. Refer to the **How To** box for hints.

1. Helen is writing a detailed report about the Wright Brothers. Which would be more useful: an encyclopedia article about airplanes or a book entitled *The Life of the Wright Brothers*? Why?

   _____
   _____
   _____

2. Rico is preparing an oral report about new developments in computers. Should he choose a magazine article published last month or an encyclopedia with a 1990 copyright date? Why?

   _____
   _____
   _____

3. LaShawn has one day to prepare a brief report about the city of Tokyo. Should she use the articles in several encyclopedias or read a 250-page nonfiction book entitled *Japan: Past and Present*? Why?

   _____
   _____

## What Have I Learned?

Suppose you were writing a detailed report about the ancient Maya. Your report should explain who the Maya were, where they lived, and how the city of Chichén Itzá looked. Describe at least three resources you would use to find this information. Tell what you would expect to learn from each resource.

# REVIEW: Using Dictionaries and Book Parts

**LESSONS 1–4**

## Reviewing What You Learned

Read each question carefully. Then circle the letter in front of the correct answer.

1. Which part of a dictionary entry tells how to say a word?
   **a.** pronunciation   **b.** index   **c.** word history

2. What do the abbreviations *v., n.,* and *adj.* tell about a word?
   **a.** its part of speech   **b.** its history   **c.** its pronunciation

3. What information can be found in every fiction and nonfiction book?
   **a.** table of contents   **b.** glossary   **c.** title information

4. Where would you look to find the meaning of a word in a nonfiction book?
   **a.** copyright page   **b.** table of contents   **c.** glossary

5. Where would you look to find out when a book was published?
   **a.** copyright page   **b.** title page   **c.** index

## Using What You Know

1. Describe two ways in which a glossary and a dictionary are similar and two ways in which they are different.
   _____
   _____
   _____

2. List four facts you can learn from title and copyright pages and a table of contents.
   _____
   _____
   _____
   _____

# REVIEW: Using Encyclopedias

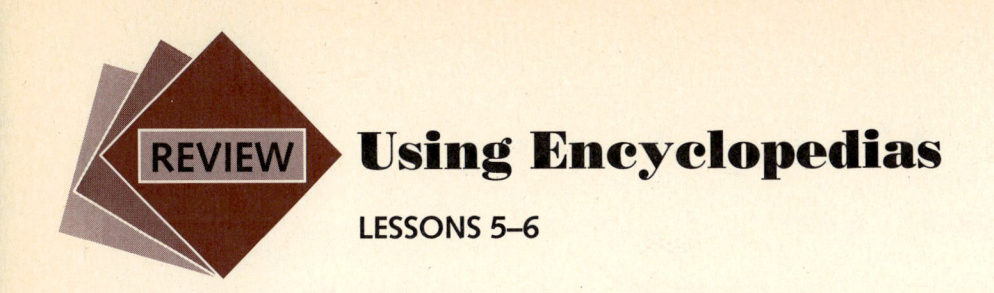

LESSONS 5–6

## Reviewing What You Learned

Complete each statement by writing in the correct answer.

1. You would use the _____ to locate topics in an encyclopedia.

2. Topics and subtopics are listed in _____ order in an encyclopedia's index.

3. The _____ at the top of an encyclopedia page tell the first and last topic on that page.

4. To find related topics in a book's index or an encyclopedia's index, you would look for _____.

5. To find an encyclopedia cross-reference marked **E:22**, you would choose volume _____.

6. You would look under _____ first to find an encyclopedia article about Nova Scotia.

7. If you need to find information about the Mexican hero Benito Juárez, you would look in the volume labeled with the letter _____.

8. If the encyclopedia index lists the topics *Egypt*, *Suez Canal*, and *Nile River* together, you know that these topics are _____.

## Using What You Know

If you were researching the migration of monarch butterflies, which topic words would you look up in an encyclopedia? List three possible topic words.

_____

_____

_____

_____

31

# REVIEW: Using Library Resources

LESSONS 7–8

## Reviewing What You Learned

Write the name of the library resource in the box that you would use to locate each of the listed items.

> card catalog  almanac  atlas
> *Readers' Guide to Periodical Literature*  microfilm

1. nonfiction book about your favorite sport _____
2. map of Greece _____
3. Olympic Gold Medal winners in figure skating in 1992 _____
4. 1963 newspaper article about Martin Luther King, Jr. _____
5. list of articles written in 1988 about bears _____
6. fiction book by the author of *Life on the Mississippi* _____
7. map of ancient Egypt showing the flooding of the Nile _____
8. last three Stanley Cup winners for hockey _____

## Using What You Know

Suppose that you had to write a detailed report about the ancient Roman city of Pompeii. Describe three resources you would choose. Explain why you would choose them.

_____
_____
_____
_____
_____
_____
_____